يس

Yā-Sin
and وَ
Al-Rahmān

الرَّحْمٰنُ

مكتبة
DAR AL TAQWA
LTD
دار التقوى

ISBN 1 870582 005

Reprinted : July 1999 / Rabi Al-Thani 1420

Published by:
Dar Al Taqwa Ltd.
7A Melcombe Street
Baker Street
London
NW1 6AE

Printed by : De-luxe Printers, London NW10 7NR. Tel : 0181 965 1771.

بسم الله الرحمن الرحیم

In the name of Allah, All-Merciful and Compassionate

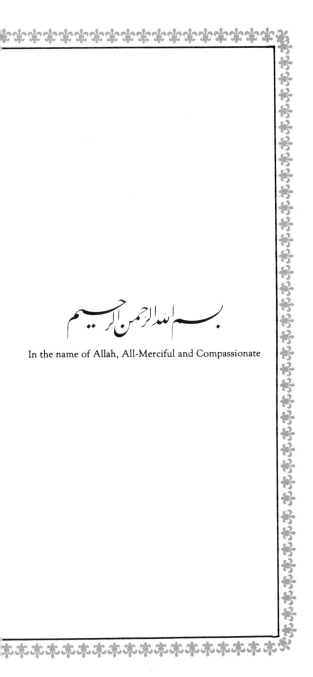

Ya-Sīn

In the name of Allah, Most Gracious,
Most Merciful.

1. **Ya - Sīn.**

2. By the Qur-ān,
Full of Wisdom,–

3. Thou art indeed
One of the messengers,

4. On a Straight Way.

5. (It is a Revelation)
Sent down by (Him),
The Exalted in Might,
Most Merciful,

6. In order that thou mayest
Warn a people,
Whose fathers were
Not warned, and who
Therefore remain heedless
(Of the Signs of Allah).

7. The Word is proved true
Against the greater part of them:
For they do not believe.

8. We have put yokes
Round their necks
Right up to their chins,
So that they cannot bow
Their heads.

سُوْرَةُ يٰسٓ مَكِّيَّةٌ، اٰيَاتُهَا ٨٣، كَلِمٰتُهَا ٧٢٩، حُرُوْفُهَا ٣٠٠٠، رُكُوْعَاتُهَا

بِسْمِ اللّٰهِ الرَّحْمٰنِ الرَّحِيْمِ

Bismi-Llaahir-Raḥmaanir-Raḥiim

يٰسٓ ۝١

Yaa Siiin

وَالْقُرْاٰنِ الْحَكِيْمِ ۝٢

wal-Qur'aanil-ḥakiim

اِنَّكَ لَمِنَ الْمُرْسَلِيْنَ ۝٣

'innaka laminal-mursaliin

عَلٰى صِرَاطٍ مُّسْتَقِيْمٍ ۝٤

'alaa ṣirātim-mustaqiim

تَنْزِيْلَ الْعَزِيْزِ الرَّحِيْمِ ۝٥

tanziilal-'Aziizir-Raḥiim

لِتُنْذِرَ قَوْمًا مَّآ اُنْذِرَ اٰبَآؤُهُمْ فَهُمْ غٰفِلُوْنَ ۝٦

litun͟dhira qawmam maaa 'un͟dhira
aabaaa'uhum fa-hum g͟haafiluun

لَقَدْ حَقَّ الْقَوْلُ عَلٰٓى اَكْثَرِهِمْ فَهُمْ لَا يُؤْمِنُوْنَ ۝٧

laqad ḥaqqal-qawlu 'alaaa 'akt͟harihim fa-
hum laa yu'minuun

اِنَّا جَعَلْنَا فِيْٓ اَعْنَاقِهِمْ اَغْلٰلًا فَهِيَ اِلَى الْاَذْقَانِ فَهُمْ مُّقْمَحُوْنَ ۝

'innaa ja'alnaa fiii 'a'naaqihim 'ag͟hlaalan fa-
hiya 'ilal-'ad͟hqani fa-hum muqmaḥuun

9. And We have put
A bar in front of them
And a bar behind them,
And further, We have
Covered them up; so that
They cannot see.

10. The same is to them
Whether thou admonish them
Or thou do not admonish
Them: they will not believe.

11. Thou canst but admonish
Such a one as follows
The Message and fears
The Most Gracious, unseen:
Give such a one, therefore,
Good tidings, of Forgiveness
And a Reward most generous.

12. Verily We shall give life
To the dead, and We record
That which they send before
And that which they leave
Behind, and of all things
Have We taken account.
In a clear Book
(Of evidence).

SECTION 2.

13. Set forth to them,
By way of a parable,
The (story of) the Companions
Of the City. Behold,
There came messengers to it.

وَجَعَلْنَا مِنۢ بَيْنِ اَيْدِيْهِمْ سَدًّا وَّمِنْ خَلْفِهِمْ سَدًّا
فَاَغْشَيْنٰهُمْ فَهُمْ لَا يُبْصِرُوْنَ ⑨

wa ja'alnaa mim-bayni 'aydiihim saddaw-
wa min khalfihim saddan fa'aghshaynaahum
fahum laa yubṣiruun

وَسَوَآءٌ عَلَيْهِمْ ءَاَنْذَرْتَهُمْ اَمْ لَمْ تُنْذِرْهُمْ لَا يُؤْمِنُوْنَ (

). wa sawaaa'un 'alayhim 'a'andhartahum 'am
lam tundhirhum laaa yu'minuun

اِنَّمَا تُنْذِرُ مَنِ اتَّبَعَ الذِّكْرَ وَخَشِيَ الرَّحْمٰنَ بِالْغَيْبِ ج
فَبَشِّرْهُ بِمَغْفِرَةٍ وَّاَجْرٍ كَرِيْمٍ ⑪

. 'innamaa tundhiru manittiba'adh-dhikra wa
khashiyar-Raḥmaana bil-ghaybi fa-
bashshirhu bi-maghfiratiw-wa 'ajrin kariim

اِنَّا نَحْنُ نُحْيِ الْمَوْتٰى وَنَكْتُبُ مَا قَدَّمُوْا وَاٰثَارَهُمْ
وَكُلَّ شَيْءٍ اَحْصَيْنٰهُ فِيْٓ اِمَامٍ مُّبِيْنٍ ⑫ ع

2. 'innaa naḥnu nuḥyil-mawtaa wa naktubu
maa qaddamuu wa 'aathaarahum wa kulla
shay'in 'aḥṣaynaahu fiii 'imaamim mubiin

(Section 2).

وقف لازم
وَاضْرِبْ لَهُمْ مَّثَلًا اَصْحٰبَ الْقَرْيَةِ ۘ اِذْ جَآءَهَا الْمُرْسَلُوْ

3. wa-ḍrib lahum mathalan 'aṣ-ḥaabal-qaryati
'idh jaaa'ahal-mursaluun

14. When We (first) sent
To them two messengers,
They rejected them:
But We strengthened them
With a third: they said,
"Truly, we have been sent
On a mission to you."

15. The (people) said: "Ye are
Only men like ourselves;
And The Most Gracious
Sends no sort of revelation:
Ye do nothing but lie."

16. They said: "Our Lord doth
Know that we have been sent
On a mission to you:

17. "And our duty is only
To deliver the clear Message."

18. The (people) said: "For us,
We augur an evil omen
From you: if ye desist not,
We will certainly stone you,
And a grievous punishment
Indeed will be inflicted
On you by us."

إِذْ أَرْسَلْنَا إِلَيْهِمُ اثْنَيْنِ فَكَذَّبُوهُمَا فَعَزَّزْنَا بِثَالِثٍ
فَقَالُوا إِنَّا إِلَيْكُم مُّرْسَلُونَ ﴿١٤﴾

idh 'arsalnaaa 'ilayhimuthnayni fa-kadhdhabuuhumaa fa-'azzaznaa bi-thaalithin fa-qaaluuu 'innaaa 'ilaykum mursaluun

قَالُوا مَا أَنتُمْ إِلَّا بَشَرٌ مِّثْلُنَا وَمَا أَنزَلَ الرَّحْمَٰنُ مِن شَ
إِنْ أَنتُمْ إِلَّا تَكْذِبُونَ ﴿١٥﴾

qaaluu maaa 'antum 'illaa basharum mithlunaa wa maaa 'anzalar-Raḥmaanu min shay'in 'in 'antum 'illaa takdhibuun

قَالُوا رَبُّنَا يَعْلَمُ إِنَّا إِلَيْكُمْ لَمُرْسَلُونَ ﴿١٦﴾

qaaluu Rabbunaa ya'lamu 'innaaa 'ilaykum la-mursaluun

وَمَا عَلَيْنَا إِلَّا الْبَلَاغُ الْمُبِينُ ﴿١٧﴾

wa maa 'alaynaaa 'illal-balaaghul-mubiin

قَالُوا إِنَّا تَطَيَّرْنَا بِكُمْ لَئِن لَّمْ تَنتَهُوا لَنَرْجُمَنَّكُمْ
وَلَيَمَسَّنَّكُم مِّنَّا عَذَابٌ أَلِيمٌ ﴿١٨﴾

qaaluuu 'innaa taṭayyarnaa bi-kum la-'illam tantahuu la-narjumannakum wa la yamassannakum min-naa 'adhaabun 'aliim

19. They said: "Your evil omens
Are with yourselves:
(Deem ye this an evil omen).
If ye are admonished?
Nay, but ye are a people
Transgressing all bounds!"

20. Then there came running,
From the farthest part
Of the City, a man,
Saying, "O my People!
Obey the messengers:

21. "Obey those who ask
No reward of you
(For themselves), and who are
Themselves guided.

22. "Why should not I
Serve Him Who created me,
And to Whom ye shall
(All) be brought back.

23. "Shall I take (other) gods
Besides Him? If The
Most Gracious should
Intend some adversity for me,
Of no use whatever
Will be their intercession
For me, nor can they
Deliver me.

24. "I would indeed, then
Be in manifest Error.

قَالُوا طَائِرُكُم مَّعَكُمْ أَئِن ذُكِّرْتُم بَلْ أَنتُمْ قَوْمٌ
مُّسْرِفُونَ ١٩

9. qaaluu ṭaaa'irukum-ma'akum 'a'in <u>dh</u>ukkirtum bal 'antum qawmum-musrifuun

وَجَاءَ مِنْ أَقْصَا الْمَدِينَةِ رَجُلٌ يَسْعَىٰ قَالَ يَا قَوْمِ اتَّبِعُوا
الْمُرْسَلِينَ ٢٠

0. wa jaaa'a min 'aqṣal-madiinati rajuluy-yas'aa qaala yaa qawmittabi'ul-mursaliin

اتَّبِعُوا مَن لَّا يَسْأَلُكُمْ أَجْرًا وَهُم مُّهْتَدُونَ ٢١

21. 'ittabi'uu mal-laa yas'alukum 'ajranw-wa hum muhtaduun

وَمَا لِيَ لَا أَعْبُدُ الَّذِي فَطَرَنِي وَإِلَيْهِ تُرْجَعُونَ ٢٢

2. wa maa liya laaa 'a'budulla<u>dh</u>ii faṭaranii wa 'ilayhi turja'uun

أَأَتَّخِذُ مِن دُونِهِ آلِهَةً إِن يُرِدْنِ الرَّحْمَٰنُ بِضُرٍّ لَّا تُغْنِ
عَنِّي شَفَاعَتُهُمْ شَيْئًا وَلَا يُنقِذُونِ ٢٣

23. 'a-'atta<u>kh</u>i<u>dh</u>u min duunihi 'aalihatan 'iy-yuridnir-Raḥmaanu bi-ḍurril-laa tug<u>h</u>ni 'annii <u>sh</u>afaa'atuhum <u>sh</u>ay'aw-wa laa yunqi<u>dh</u>uun

إِنِّي إِذًا لَّفِي ضَلَالٍ مُّبِينٍ ٢٤

24. 'inniii 'i<u>dh</u>al-la-fii ḍalaalim-mubiin

25. "For me, I have faith
In the Lord of you (all):
Listen, then, to me!"

26 It was said: "Enter thou
The Garden." He said:
"Ah me! Would that
My People knew (what I know)!–

27. "From That my Lord
Has granted me Forgiveness
And has enrolled me
Among those held in honour!"

28. And We sent not down
Against his People, after him,
Any hosts from heaven,
Nor was it needful
For Us so to do.

29. It was no more than
A single mighty Blast,
And behold! they were
(like ashes)
Quenched and silent.

30. Ah! alas for the servants!
There comes not a messenger
To them but they mock him!

31. See they not how many
Generations before them
We destroyed? Not to them
Will they return:

إِنِّيٓ ءَامَنتُ بِرَبِّكُمۡ فَٱسۡمَعُونِ ٢٥

25. 'inniii 'aamantu bi-Rabbikum fa-sma'uun

قِيلَ ٱدۡخُلِ ٱلۡجَنَّةَۖ قَالَ يَٰلَيۡتَ قَوۡمِي يَعۡلَمُونَ ٢٦

26. qiila-dkhulil-janna qaala yaa-layta qawmii
ya'lamuun

بِمَا غَفَرَ لِي رَبِّي وَجَعَلَنِي مِنَ ٱلۡمُكۡرَمِينَ ٢٧

27. bi-maa ghafara lii Rabii wa ja'alanii minal-
mukramiin

وَمَآ أَنزَلۡنَا عَلَىٰ قَوۡمِهِۦ مِنۢ بَعۡدِهِۦ مِن جُندٖ مِّنَ ٱلسَّمَآءِ
وَمَا كُنَّا مُنزِلِينَ ٢٨

28. wa maaa 'anzalnaa 'alaa qawmihi mim-
ba'dihi min jundim-minas- samaaa'i wa maa
kunnaa munziliin

إِن كَانَتۡ إِلَّا صَيۡحَةٗ وَٰحِدَةٗ فَإِذَا هُمۡ خَٰمِدُونَ ٢٩

29. 'in kaanat 'illaa ṣayḥataw-waaḥidatan fa-
'idhaa hum khaamiduun

يَٰحَسۡرَةً عَلَى ٱلۡعِبَادِۚ مَا يَأۡتِيهِم مِّن رَّسُولٍ إِلَّا كَانُواْ بِهِۦ
يَسۡتَهۡزِءُونَ ٣٠

وقف غفران

30. yaa-ḥasratan 'alal-'ibaad maa ya'tiihim mir-
rasuulin 'illaa kaanuu bihi yastahzi'uun

أَلَمۡ يَرَوۡاْ كَمۡ أَهۡلَكۡنَا قَبۡلَهُم مِّنَ ٱلۡقُرُونِ أَنَّهُمۡ إِلَيۡهِمۡ لَا يَرۡجِعُونَ

31. 'a-lam yaraw kam 'ahlaknaa qablahum
minal-quruuni 'annahum 'ilayhim laa
yarji'uun

32. But each one of them
All–will be brought
Before Us (for judgment).

SECTION 3.

33. A Sign for them
Is the earth that is dead:
We do give it life,
And produce grain therefrom,
Of which ye do eat.

34. And We produce therein
Orchards with date-palms
And vines, and We cause
Springs to gush forth therein:

35. That they may enjoy
The fruits of this (artistry):
It was not their hands
That made this:
Will they not then give thanks?

36. Glory to Allah, Who created
In pairs all things that
The earth produces, as well as
Their own (human) kind
And (other) things of which
They have no knowledge.

37. And a Sign for them
Is the Night: We withdraw
Therefrom the Day, and behold
They are plunged in darkness;

وَاِنْ كُلٌّ لَّمَّا جَمِيْعٌ لَّدَيْنَا مُحْضَرُوْنَ ﴿٣٢﴾

?. wa 'in kullul-lammaa jamii'ul-ladaynaa muḥḍaruuun

وَاٰيَةٌ لَّهُمُ الْاَرْضُ الْمَيْتَةُ ۖ اَحْيَيْنٰهَا وَاَخْرَجْنَا مِنْهَا حَبًّا فَمِنْهُ يَاْكُلُوْنَ ﴿٣٣﴾

?. wa 'aayatul-lahumul-'arḍul-maytatu 'aḥyaynaahaa wa 'akhrajnaa minhaa ḥabban fa-minhu ya'kuluun

وَجَعَلْنَا فِيْهَا جَنّٰتٍ مِّنْ نَّخِيْلٍ وَّاَعْنَابٍ وَّفَجَّرْنَا فِيْهَا مِنَ الْعُيُوْنِ

4. wa ja'alnaa fiihaa jannaatim-min nakhiiliw-wa 'a'naabiw-wa fajjarnaa fiihaa minal-'uyuun

لِيَاْكُلُوْا مِنْ ثَمَرِهٖ ۙ وَمَا عَمِلَتْهُ اَيْدِيْهِمْ ۗ اَفَلَا يَشْكُرُوْنَ ﴿

5. li-ya'kuluu min thamarihii wa maa 'amilat-hu aydiihim 'a-fa-laa yashkuruun

سُبْحٰنَ الَّذِيْ خَلَقَ الْاَزْوَاجَ كُلَّهَا مِمَّا تُنْۢبِتُ الْاَرْضُ وَمِنْ اَ
وَمِمَّا لَا يَعْلَمُوْنَ ﴿٣٦﴾

5. subḥaanal-ladhii khalaqal-'azwaaja kullahaa mimmaatumbitul-'arḍu wa min 'anfusihim wa mim-maa laa ya'lamuun

وَاٰيَةٌ لَّهُمُ الَّيْلُ ۖ نَسْلَخُ مِنْهُ النَّهَارَ فَاِذَا هُمْ مُّظْلِمُوْنَ ﴿

7. wa 'aayatul-lahumul-laylu naslakhu minhun-nahaara fa-'idhaa hum muẓlimuun

38. And the Sun
Runs unto a resting place,
For him: that is
The decree of (Him),
The Exalted in Might,
The All-Knowing.

39. And the Moon,–
We have measured for her
Stations (to traverse)
Till she returns
Like the old (and withered)
Lower part of a date-stalk.

40. It is not permitted
To the Sun to catch up
The Moon, nor can
The Night outstrip the Day:
Each (just) swims along
In (its own) orbit
(According to Law).

41. And a Sign for them
Is that We bore
Their race (through the Flood)
In the loaded Ark;

42. And We have created
For them similar (vessels)
On which they ride.

وَالشَّمْسُ تَجْرِىْ لِمُسْتَقَرٍّ لَّهَا ؕ ذٰلِكَ تَقْدِيْرُ الْعَزِيْزِ الْعَلِيْمِ

8. wash-shamsu tajrii li-mustaqarril-lahaa
dhaalika taqdiirul-'Aziizil-'Aliim

وَالْقَمَرَ قَدَّرْنٰهُ مَنَازِلَ حَتّٰى عَادَ كَالْعُرْجُوْنِ الْقَدِيْمِ ﴿٣٩﴾

39. wal-qamara qaddarnaahu manaazila ḥattaa
'aada kal-'urjuunil-qadiim

لَا الشَّمْسُ يَنْۢبَغِىْ لَهَآ اَنْ تُدْرِكَ الْقَمَرَ وَلَا الَّيْلُ
سَابِقُ النَّهَارِ ؕ وَ كُلٌّ فِىْ فَلَكٍ يَّسْبَحُوْنَ ﴿٤٠﴾

40. lash-shamsu yambaghii lahaaa 'an tudrikal-
qamarawa lal-laylu saabiqun-nahaar wa
kullun fii falakiy-yasbaḥuun

وَ اٰيَةٌ لَّهُمْ اَنَّا حَمَلْنَا ذُرِّيَّتَهُمْ فِى الْفُلْكِ الْمَشْحُوْنِ ﴿٤١﴾

41. wa 'aayatul-lahum 'annaa ḥamalnaa
dhurriyyatahum fil-fulkil-mashḥuun

وَخَلَقْنَا لَهُمْ مِّنْ مِّثْلِهٖ مَا يَرْكَبُوْنَ ﴿٤٢﴾

42. wa khalaqnaa lahum mim-mithlihii maa
yarkabuun

43. If it were Our Will,
We could drown them:
Then would there be
No helper (to hear
Their cry), nor could
They be delivered,

44. Except by way of Mercy
From Us, and by way
Of (worldly) convenience
(To serve them) for a time.

45. When they are told,
"Fear ye that which is
Before you and that which
Will be after you, in order
That ye may receive Mercy,"
(They turn back).

46. Not a Sign comes to them
From among the Signs
Of their Lord, but they
Turn away therefrom.

47. And when they are told,
"Spend ye of (the bounties)
With which Allah
Has provided you," the Unbelievers
Say to those who believe:
"Shall we then feed those
Whom, if Allah had so willed,
He would have fed, (Himself)?–
Ye are in nothing
But manifest error."

وَإِن نَّشَأْ نُغْرِقْهُمْ فَلَا صَرِيخَ لَهُمْ وَلَا هُمْ يُنقَذُونَ ﴿٤٣﴾

3. wa 'in na<u>sh</u>a' nu<u>gh</u>riqhum fa-laa ṣarii<u>kh</u>a lahum wa laa hum yunqa<u>dh</u>uun

إِلَّا رَحْمَةً مِّنَّا وَمَتَاعًا إِلَىٰ حِينٍ ﴿٤٤﴾

4. 'illaa raḥmatam-minnaa wa mataa'an ilaa ḥiin

وَإِذَا قِيلَ لَهُمُ اتَّقُوا مَا بَيْنَ أَيْدِيكُمْ وَمَا خَلْفَكُمْ لَعَلَّكُمْ
تُرْحَمُونَ ﴿٤٥﴾

5. wa 'i<u>dh</u>aa qiila lahumu-ttaquu maa bayna 'aydiikum wa maa <u>kh</u>alfakum la'allakum turḥamuun

وَمَا تَأْتِيهِم مِّنْ آيَةٍ مِّنْ آيَاتِ رَبِّهِمْ إِلَّا كَانُوا عَنْهَا مُعْرِضِينَ

6. wa maa ta'tiihim min 'ayyatim-min 'aayaati Rabbihim 'illaa kaanuu 'anhaa mu'riḍiin

وَإِذَا قِيلَ لَهُمْ أَنفِقُوا مِمَّا رَزَقَكُمُ اللَّهُ قَالَ الَّذِينَ كَفَرُوا لِلَّذِينَ
آمَنُوا أَنُطْعِمُ مَن لَّوْ يَشَاءُ اللَّهُ أَطْعَمَهُ إِنْ أَنتُمْ إِلَّا فِي
ضَلَالٍ مُّبِينٍ ﴿٤٧﴾

7. wa 'i<u>dh</u>aa qiila lahum 'anfiquu mimmaa razaqakumu-Llaahu qaalal-la<u>dh</u>iina kafaruu lil-la<u>dh</u>iina 'aamanuuu 'anuṭ'imu mal-law ya<u>sh</u>aaa'u-Llaahu 'aṭ'amahu 'in 'antum 'illaa fii ḍalaalim-mubiin

48. Further, they say, "When
Will this promise (come to pass),
If what ye say is true?"

49. They will not (have
To) wait for aught
But a single Blast:
It will seize them while
They are yet disputing
Among themselves!

50. No (chance) will they then
Have, by will, to dispose
(Of their affairs), nor
To return to their own people!

SECTION 4.

51. The trumpet shall be
Sounded, when behold!
From the sepulchres (men)
Will rush forth
To their Lord!

52. They will say: "Ah!
Woe unto us! Who
Hath raised us up
From our beds of repose?"...
(A voice will say:)
"This is what The
Most Gracious had promised.
And true was the word
Of the messengers!"

وَيَقُولُونَ مَتَىٰ هَٰذَا الْوَعْدُ إِن كُنتُمْ صَادِقِينَ ﴿٤٨﴾

8. wa yaquuluuna matta haadhal-wa‘du ’in
kun-tum ṣaadiqiin

مَا يَنظُرُونَ إِلَّا صَيْحَةً وَاحِدَةً تَأْخُذُهُمْ وَهُمْ يَخِصِّمُونَ

9. maa yanẓuruuna ’illaa ṣayḥataw-waaḥidatan
ta’khudhuhum wa hum yakhiṣṣimuun

فَلَا يَسْتَطِيعُونَ تَوْصِيَةً وَلَا إِلَىٰ أَهْلِهِمْ يَرْجِعُونَ ﴿٥٠﴾

0. fa-laa yastaṭii‘uuna tawṣiyataw-wa laaa ’ilaa
’ahlihim yarji‘uun

وَنُفِخَ فِي الصُّورِ فَإِذَا هُم مِّنَ الْأَجْدَاثِ إِلَىٰ رَبِّهِمْ يَنسِلُونَ

1. wa nufikha fiṣ-ṣuuri fa-’idhaa hum minal-
’ajdaathi ilaa Rabbihim yan-siluun

قَالُوا يَا وَيْلَنَا مَن بَعَثَنَا مِن مَّرْقَدِنَا ۜ هَٰذَا مَا وَعَدَ
الرَّحْمَٰنُ وَصَدَقَ الْمُرْسَلُونَ ﴿٥٢﴾

2. qaaluu yaa-waylanaa mam-ba‘athanaa mim-
marqadinaa haadhaa maa wa‘adar-
Raḥmaanu wa ṣadaqal-mursaluun

53. It will be no more
Than a single Blast,
When lo! they will all
Be brought up before Us!

54. Then, on that Day,
Not a soul will be
Wronged in the least,
And ye shall but
Be repaid the meeds
Of your past Deeds.

55. Verily the Companions
Of the Garden shall
That Day have joy
In all that they do;

56. They and their associates
Will be in pleasant
Shade, reclining
On raised couches;

57. (Every) fruit
Will be there for them;
They shall have whatever
They call· for;

58. "Peace!"–a Word
(Of salutation) from a Lord
Most Merciful!

59. "And O ye in sin!
Get ye apart this Day!

إِن كَانَتْ إِلَّا صَيْحَةً وَاحِدَةً فَإِذَا هُمْ جَمِيعٌ لَّدَيْنَا مُحْضَرُونَ

53. 'in kaanat 'illaa ṣayḥataw-waaḥidatan fa-'idhaa hum jamii'ul-ladaynaa muḥḍaruun

فَالْيَوْمَ لَا تُظْلَمُ نَفْسٌ شَيْئًا وَلَا تُجْزَوْنَ إِلَّا مَا كُنتُمْ تَعْمَلُونَ

54. fal-yawma laa tuẓlamu nafsun shay'aw-walaa tujzawna 'illaa maa kun-tum ta'maluun

إِنَّ أَصْحَابَ الْجَنَّةِ الْيَوْمَ فِي شُغُلٍ فَاكِهُونَ ٥٥

55. 'inna 'aṣ-ḥaabal-jannatil-yawma fii shughulin faakihuun

هُمْ وَأَزْوَاجُهُمْ فِي ظِلَالٍ عَلَى الْأَرَائِكِ مُتَّكِئُونَ ٥٦

56. hum wa 'azwaajuhum fii ẓilaalin 'alal-'araaa'iki muttaki'uun

لَهُمْ فِيهَا فَاكِهَةٌ وَلَهُمْ مَا يَدَّعُونَ ٥٧

57. lahum fiihaa faakihatuw-wa lahum maa yadda'uun

سَلَامٌ قَوْلًا مِّن رَّبٍّ رَّحِيمٍ ٥٨

58. salaamun qawlam-mir-Rabbir-Raḥiim

وَامْتَازُوا الْيَوْمَ أَيُّهَا الْمُجْرِمُونَ ٥٩

59. wamtaazul-yawma 'ayyuhal-mujrimuun

60. "Did I not enjoin
On you, O ye children
Of Adam, that ye
Should not worship Satan;
For that he was to you
An enemy avowed?–.

61. "And that ye should
Worship Me, (for that) this
Was the Straight Way?

62. "But he did lead astray
A great multitude of you.
Did ye not, then, understand?

63. "This is the Hell
Of which ye were promised

64. "Embrace ye the (Fire)
This Day, for that ye
(Persistently) rejected (Truth)."

65. That Day shall We set
A seal on their mouths.
But their hands will speak
To Us, and their feet
Bear witness, to all
That they did.

66. If it had been Our Will,
We could surely have
Blotted out their eyes;
Then they should have
Raced to the Path,
But how could they have seen?

أَلَمْ أَعْهَدْ إِلَيْكُمْ يَٰبَنِىٓ ءَادَمَ أَن لَّا تَعْبُدُوا الشَّيْطَٰنَ ۖ إِنَّهُ لَكُمْ عَدُوٌّ مُّبِينٌ ٦٠

0. 'a-lam a'had 'ilaykum yaa Baniii 'Aadama 'al-laa ta'budush-Shaytaan\ 'innahu lakum 'aduwwum-mubiin

وَأَنِ اعْبُدُونِى ۚ هَٰذَا صِرَٰطٌ مُّسْتَقِيمٌ ٦١ وقف غفران

1. wa 'ani'buduunii\ haadhaa ṣiraaṭum-mustaqiim

وَلَقَدْ أَضَلَّ مِنكُمْ جِبِلًّا كَثِيرًا ۖ أَفَلَمْ تَكُونُوا تَعْقِلُونَ

2. wa laqad 'aḍalla min-kum jibillan kathiira 'a-fa-lam takuunuu ta'qiluun

هَٰذِهِ جَهَنَّمُ الَّتِى كُنتُمْ تُوعَدُونَ ٦٣

3. haadhihi jahannamul-latii kun-tum tuu'aduun

اصْلَوْهَا الْيَوْمَ بِمَا كُنتُمْ تَكْفُرُونَ ٦٤

4. 'iṣlawhal-yawma bi-maa kun-tum takfuruun

الْيَوْمَ نَخْتِمُ عَلَىٰٓ أَفْوَٰهِهِمْ وَتُكَلِّمُنَآ أَيْدِيهِمْ وَتَشْهَدُ أَرْجُلُهُم بِمَا كَانُوا يَكْسِبُونَ ٦٥

5. 'al-yawma nakhtimu 'alaaa 'afwaahihim wa tukallimunaaa 'aydiihim wa tashhadu 'arjuluhum bimaa kaanuu yaksibuun

وَلَوْ نَشَآءُ لَطَمَسْنَا عَلَىٰٓ أَعْيُنِهِمْ فَاسْتَبَقُوا الصِّرَٰطَ فَأَنَّىٰ يُبْصِرُونَ

6. wa law nashaaa'u la-ṭamasnaa 'alaaa a'yunihim fa-stabaquṣ-ṣiraaṭa fa-'annaa yubṣiruun

67. And if it had been
Our Will, We could
Have transformed them
In their places;
Then should they have been
Unable to move about,
Nor could they have returned
(After error).

SECTION 5.

68. If We grant long life
To any, We cause him
To be reversed in nature:
Will they not then understand?

69. We have not instructed
The (Prophet) in Poetry,
Nor is it meet for him:
This is no less than
A Message and a Qur-ān
Making things clear:

70. That it may give admonition
To any (who are) alive,
And that the word
May be proved true against those
Who reject (Truth).

71. See they not that it is
We Who have created
For them–among the things
Which our hands have fashioned–
Cattle, which are under
Their dominion?–

ع وَلَوْ نَشَآءُ لَمَسَخْنٰهُمْ عَلٰى مَكَانَتِهِمْ فَمَا اسْتَطَاعُوْا مُضِيًّا
وَّلَا يَرْجِعُوْنَ ﴿٦٧﴾

67. wa law na<u>sh</u>aaa'u la-masa<u>kh</u>naahum 'alaa makaanatihim fa-mastaṭaa'uu muḍiyyaw-wa laa yarji'uun

(Section 5).

وَمَنْ نُّعَمِّرْهُ نُنَكِّسْهُ فِي الْخَلْقِ ۗ اَفَلَا يَعْقِلُوْنَ ﴿٦٨﴾

68. wa man nu'ammirhu nunakkis-hu fil-<u>kh</u>alq 'a-fa-laa ya'qiluun

وَمَا عَلَّمْنٰهُ الشِّعْرَ وَمَا يَنْۢبَغِيْ لَهٗ ۗ اِنْ هُوَ اِلَّا ذِكْرٌ وَّقُرْاٰنٌ مُّبِيْنٌ

69. wa maa 'allamnaahu<u>sh</u>-<u>sh</u>i'ra wa maa yambag<u>h</u>ii lah 'in huwa 'illaa <u>dh</u>ikruw-wa Qur'aanum-mubiin

لِّيُنْذِرَ مَنْ كَانَ حَيًّا وَّيَحِقَّ الْقَوْلُ عَلَى الْكٰفِرِيْنَ ﴿٧٠﴾

70. li-yun<u>dh</u>ira man kaana ḥayyaw-wa yaḥiqqal-qawlu 'alal-kaafiriin

اَوَلَمْ يَرَوْا اَنَّا خَلَقْنَا لَهُمْ مِّمَّا عَمِلَتْ اَيْدِيْنَآ اَنْعَامًا فَهُمْ
لَهَا مٰلِكُوْنَ ﴿٧١﴾

71. a-wa lam yaraw 'annaa <u>kh</u>alaqnaa lahum mimmaa 'amilat 'aydiinaaa 'an'ammaan fa-hum lahaa maalikuun

72. And that We have
Subjected them to their (use)?
Of them some do carry them
And some they eat:

73. And they have (other) profits
From them (besides), and they
Get (milk) to drink.
Will they not then
Be grateful?

74. Yet they take (for worship)
Gods other than Allah,
(Hoping) that they might
Be helped!

75. They have not the power
To help them: and
They are a host
Brought up before them.

76. Let not their speech, then,
Grieve thee. Verily We know
What they hide as well as
What they disclose.

77. **D**oth not man see
That it is We Who
Created him from sperm?
Yet behold! he (stands forth)
As an open adversary!

وَذَلَّلْنَٰهَا لَهُمْ فَمِنْهَا رَكُوبُهُمْ وَمِنْهَا يَأْكُلُونَ ﴿٧٢﴾

72. wa dhallalnaahaa lahum fa-minhaa rakuubuhum wa minhaa ya'kuluun

وَلَهُمْ فِيهَا مَنَٰفِعُ وَمَشَارِبُ ۖ أَفَلَا يَشْكُرُونَ ﴿٧٣﴾

73. wa lahum fiihaa manaafi‘u wa mashaarib 'a-fa-laa yashkuruun

وَٱتَّخَذُوا۟ مِن دُونِ ٱللَّهِ ءَالِهَةً لَّعَلَّهُمْ يُنصَرُونَ ﴿٧٤﴾

74. wattakhadhuu min duuni-Llaahi 'aalihatal-la‘allahum yunṣaruun

لَا يَسْتَطِيعُونَ نَصْرَهُمْ وَهُمْ لَهُمْ جُندٌ مُّحْضَرُونَ ﴿٧٥﴾

75. laa yastaṭii‘uuna naṣrahum wa hum lahum jundum-muḥḍaruun

فَلَا يَحْزُنكَ قَوْلُهُمْ ۘ إِنَّا نَعْلَمُ مَا يُسِرُّونَ وَمَا يُعْلِنُونَ ﴿٧٦﴾

76. fa-laa yahzun-ka qawluhum innaa na‘lamu maa yusirruuna wa maa yu‘linuun

أَوَلَمْ يَرَ ٱلْإِنسَٰنُ أَنَّا خَلَقْنَٰهُ مِن نُّطْفَةٍ فَإِذَا هُوَ خَصِيمٌ مُّبِينٌ

77. 'a-wa lam yaral-'insaanu 'annaa khalaqnaahu min nuṭfatin fa-'idhaa huwa khaṣiimum-mubiin

78. And he makes comparisons
For Us, and forgets his own
(Origin and) Creation:
He says, "Who can give
Life to (dry) bones
And decomposed ones (at that)?"

79. Say, "He will give them
Life Who created them
For the first time!
For He fully knows
All creation.

80 "The same Who produces
For you fire out of
The green tree, when behold!
Ye kindle therewith
(Your own fires)!

81. "Is not He Who created
The heavens and the earth
Able to create the like
Thereof?"–Yea, indeed!
For He is the Creator Supreme,
Of skill and knowledge (infinite)!

82. Verily, when He intends
A thing, His Command is,
"Be", and it is!

83. So glory to Him
In Whose Hands is
The dominion of all things:
And to Him will ye
Be all brought back.

وَضَرَبَ لَنَا مَثَلًا وَّنَسِيَ خَلْقَهٗ ۭ قَالَ مَنْ يُّحْيِ الْعِظَامَ وَهِيَ رَمِيْمٌ ۝۷۸

3. wa ḍaraba la-naa ma<u>th</u>alaw-wa nasiya <u>kh</u>alqah qaala man yuḥyil-'iẓaama wa hiya ramiim

قُلْ يُحْيِيْهَا الَّذِيْٓ اَنْشَاَهَآ اَوَّلَ مَرَّةٍ ۭ وَهُوَ بِكُلِّ خَلْقٍ عَلِيْمُۨ

9. qul yuḥyiihal-la<u>dh</u>iii 'an<u>sh</u>a'ahaaa 'awwala marra wa Huwa bi-kulli <u>kh</u>alqin 'aliim

الَّذِيْ جَعَلَ لَكُمْ مِّنَ الشَّجَرِ الْاَخْضَرِ نَارًا فَاِذَآ اَنْتُمْ مِّنْهُ تُوْقِدُوْنَ ۝۸۰

0. 'al-'la<u>dh</u>ii ja'ala la-kum mina<u>sh</u>-shajaril-'a<u>kh</u>ḍari naaran fa-'i<u>dh</u>aaa 'an-tum minhu tuuqiduun

اَوَلَيْسَ الَّذِيْ خَلَقَ السَّمٰوٰتِ وَالْاَرْضَ بِقٰدِرٍ عَلٰٓي اَنْ يَّخْلُقَ مِثْلَهُمْ ۭ بَلٰى ۤ وَهُوَ الْخَلّٰقُ الْعَلِيْمُ ۝۸۱

1. 'a-wa laysal-la<u>dh</u>ii <u>kh</u>alqas-samaawaati wal-'arḍa bi-qaadirin 'alaaa 'ay-ya<u>kh</u>luqa mi<u>th</u>lahum balaa wa Huwal-<u>Kh</u>allaaqul-'Aliim

اِنَّمَآ اَمْرُهٗٓ اِذَآ اَرَادَ شَيْـًٔا اَنْ يَّقُوْلَ لَهٗ كُنْ فَيَكُوْنُ ۝۸۲

2. 'innamaaa 'amruhuu 'i<u>dh</u>aa 'araada <u>sh</u>ay'an 'ay-yaquula lahu kun fa-yakuun

فَسُبْحٰنَ الَّذِيْ بِيَدِهٖ مَلَكُوْتُ كُلِّ شَيْءٍ وَّاِلَيْهِ تُرْجَعُوْنَ

3. fa-subḥaanal-la<u>dh</u>ii bi-yadihi malakuutu kulli <u>sh</u>ay'iw-wa 'ilayhi turja'uun

Ar-Rahmān, or (Allah) Most Gracious.

In the name of Allah, Most Gracious,
Most Merciful.

1. The Most Gracious!

2. It is He Who has
Taught the Qur-ān.

3. He has created man:

4. He has taught him
An intelligent speech.

5. The sun and the moon
Follow courses (exactly) computed;

6. And the herbs and the trees–
Both (alike) bow in adoration.

7. And the Firmament has He
Raised high, and He has set up
The Balance (of Justice),

8. In order that ye may
Not transgress (due) balance.

9. So establish weight with justice
And fall not short
In the balance.

10. It is He Who has
Spread out the earth
For (His) creatures:

سُوْرَةُ الرَّحْمٰنِ مَدَنِيَّةٌ، اٰيَاتُهَا ٧٨ كَلِمٰتُهَا ٣٥١، حُرُوْفُهَا ١٦٣٦، رُكُوْعَاتُهَا ٣

بِسْمِ اللّٰهِ الرَّحْمٰنِ الرَّحِيْمِ

Bismi-Llaahir-Raḥmaanir-Raḥiim

اَلرَّحْمٰنُ ﴿١﴾

'ar-Raḥmaan

عَلَّمَ الْقُرْاٰنَ ﴿٢﴾

'allamaal-Qur'aan

خَلَقَ الْاِنْسَانَ ﴿٣﴾

khalaqal-'insaan

عَلَّمَهُ الْبَيَانَ ﴿٤﴾

'allamahul-bayaan

اَلشَّمْسُ وَالْقَمَرُ بِحُسْبَانٍ ﴿٥﴾

'ash-shamsu wal-qamaru bi-ḥusbaan

وَّالنَّجْمُ وَالشَّجَرُ يَسْجُدٰنِ ﴿٦﴾

wan-najmu wash-shajaru yasjudaan

وَالسَّمَآءَ رَفَعَهَا وَوَضَعَ الْمِيْزَانَ ﴿٧﴾

was-samaaa'a rafa'ahaa wa-waḍa'al-miizaan

اَلَّا تَطْغَوْا فِى الْمِيْزَانِ ﴿٨﴾

'allaa taṭghaw fil-miizaan

وَاَقِيْمُوا الْوَزْنَ بِالْقِسْطِ وَلَا تُخْسِرُوا الْمِيْزَانَ ﴿٩﴾

wa 'aqiimul-wazna bil-qisṭi wa-laa tukhsirul-miizaan

وَالْاَرْضَ وَضَعَهَا لِلْاَنَامِ ﴿١٠﴾

0. wal-'arḍa wada'ahaa lil-'anaam

11. Therein is fruit
And date-palms, producing
Spathes (enclosing dates);

12. Also corn, with (its)
Leaves and stalk for fodder,
And sweet-smelling plants.

13. Then which of the favours
Of your Lord will ye deny?

14. **He** created man
From sounding clay
Like unto pottery,

15. And He created Jinns
From fire free of smoke:

16. Then which of the favours
Of your Lord will ye deny?

17. (**He** is) Lord
Of the two Easts
And Lord
Of the two Wests:

18. Then which of the favours
Of your Lord will ye deny?

19. **He** has let free
The two Seas
Meeting together:

20. Between them is a Barrier
Which they do not transgress:

21. Then which of the favours
Of your Lord will ye deny?

فِيهَا فَاكِهَةٌ وَّالنَّخْلُ ذَاتُ الْأَكْمَامِ ﴿١١﴾

. fiihaa faakihatuw-wa-n-nakhlu dhaatul-
akmaam

وَالْحَبُّ ذُو الْعَصْفِ وَالرَّيْحَانُ ﴿١٢﴾

. wal-ḥabbu dhul-'aṣfi war-rayḥaan

فَبِأَيِّ آلَاءِ رَبِّكُمَا تُكَذِّبَانِ ﴿١٣﴾

. fa-bi-'ayyi 'aalaaa'i Rabbikumaa
tukadhdhibaan

خَلَقَ الْإِنسَانَ مِن صَلْصَالٍ كَالْفَخَّارِ ﴿١٤﴾

. khalaqal-'in-saana min ṣalṣaalin kal-
fakhkhaar

وَخَلَقَ الْجَانَّ مِن مَّارِجٍ مِّن نَّارٍ ﴿١٥﴾

. wa khalaqal-jaaanna mim-maarijim-min-
naar

فَبِأَيِّ آلَاءِ رَبِّكُمَا تُكَذِّبَانِ ﴿١٦﴾

. fa-bi-'ayyi 'aalaaa'i Rabbikumaa
tukadhdhibaan

رَبُّ الْمَشْرِقَيْنِ وَرَبُّ الْمَغْرِبَيْنِ ﴿١٧﴾

. Rabbul-mashriqayni wa-Rabbul-maghribayn

فَبِأَيِّ آلَاءِ رَبِّكُمَا تُكَذِّبَانِ ﴿١٨﴾

. fa-bi-'ayyi 'aalaaa'i Rabbikumaa
tukadhdhibaan

مَرَجَ الْبَحْرَيْنِ يَلْتَقِيَانِ ﴿١٩﴾

. marajal-baḥrayni yaltaqiyaan

بَيْنَهُمَا بَرْزَخٌ لَّا يَبْغِيَانِ ﴿٢٠﴾

. baynahumaa barzakhul laa yabghiyaan

فَبِأَيِّ آلَاءِ رَبِّكُمَا تُكَذِّبَانِ ﴿٢١﴾

. fa-bi-'ayyi 'aalaaa'i Rabbikumaa
tukadhdhibaan

22. **O**ut of them come
Pearls and Coral:

23. Then which of the favours
Of your Lord will ye deny?

24. **A**nd His are the Ships
Sailing smoothly through the seas,
Lofty as mountains:

25. Then which of the favours
Of your Lord will ye deny?

SECTION 2.

26. **A**ll that is on earth
Will perish:

27. But will abide (for ever)
The Face of thy Lord,–
Full of Majesty,
Bounty and Honour.

28. Then which of the favours
Of your Lord will ye deny?

29. **O**f Him seeks (its need)
Every creature in the heavens
And on earth:
Every day in (new) Splendour
Doth He (shine)!

30. Then which of the favours
Of your Lord will ye deny?

31. **S**oon shall We
Settle your affairs,
O both ye worlds!

يَخْرُجُ مِنْهُمَا اللُّؤْلُؤُ وَالْمَرْجَانُ ﴿٢٢﴾

2. yakhruju minhumal-lu'lu'u wal-marjaan

فَبِأَيِّ آلَاءِ رَبِّكُمَا تُكَذِّبَانِ ﴿٢٣﴾

3. fa-bi-'ayyi 'aalaaa'i Rabbikumaa
tukadhdhibaan

وَلَهُ الْجَوَارِ الْمُنْشَآتُ فِي الْبَحْرِ كَالْأَعْلَامِ ﴿٢٤﴾

4. wa lahul-jawaaril-mun-sha'aatu fil-baḥri kal-'a'laam

ع فَبِأَيِّ آلَاءِ رَبِّكُمَا تُكَذِّبَانِ ﴿٢٥﴾

5. fa-bi-'ayyi 'aalaaa'i Rabbikumaa
tukadhdhibaan

كُلُّ مَنْ عَلَيْهَا فَانٍ ﴿٢٦﴾

6. kullu man 'alayhaa faan

وَيَبْقَىٰ وَجْهُ رَبِّكَ ذُو الْجَلَالِ وَالْإِكْرَامِ ﴿٢٧﴾

7. wa yabqaa Wajhu Rabbika Dhul-jalaali wal-'ikraam

فَبِأَيِّ آلَاءِ رَبِّكُمَا تُكَذِّبَانِ ﴿٢٨﴾

8. fa-bi-'ayyi 'aalaaa'i Rabbikumaa
tukadhdhibaan

يَسْأَلُهُ مَنْ فِي السَّمَاوَاتِ وَالْأَرْضِ ۚ كُلَّ يَوْمٍ هُوَ فِي شَأْنٍ ﴿٢٩﴾

9. yas'aluhu man fis-samaawaati wal-'arḍ kulla yawmin Huwa fii sha'n

فَبِأَيِّ آلَاءِ رَبِّكُمَا تُكَذِّبَانِ ﴿٣٠﴾

0. fa-bi-'ayyi 'aalaaa'i Rabbikumaa
tukadhdhibaan

سَنَفْرُغُ لَكُمْ أَيُّهَ الثَّقَلَانِ ﴿٣١﴾

1. sa-nafrughu lakum 'ayyuhath-thaqalaan

32. Then which of the favours
Of your Lord will ye deny?

33. **O** ye assembly of Jinns
And men! If it be
Ye can pass beyond
The zones of the heavens
And the earth, pass ye!
Not without authority
Shall ye be able to pass!

34. Then which of the favours
Of your Lord will ye deny?

35. **On** you will be sent
(O ye evil ones twain!)
A flame of fire (to burn)
And a (flash of) molten brass
No defence will ye have:

36. Then which of the favours
Of your Lord will ye deny?

37. When the sky is rent
Asunder, and it becomes red
Like ointment:

38. Then which of the favours
Of your Lord will ye deny?

39. On that Day
No question will be asked
Of man or Jinn
As to his sin,

40. Then which of the favours
Of your Lord will ye deny?

فَبِأَيِّ آلَاءِ رَبِّكُمَا تُكَذِّبَانِ ﴿٣٢﴾

2. fa-bi-'ayyi 'aalaaa'i Rabbikumaa
tukadhdhibaan

يَا مَعْشَرَ الْجِنِّ وَالْإِنسِ إِنِ اسْتَطَعْتُمْ أَن تَنفُذُوا مِنْ أَقْطَارِ
السَّمَاوَاتِ وَالْأَرْضِ فَانفُذُوا ۚ لَا تَنفُذُونَ إِلَّا بِسُلْطَانٍ ﴿٣٣﴾

3. yaa-ma'sharal-jinni wal-'insi 'inistata'tum
'an tan-fudhuu min 'aqṭaaris-samaawaati
wal-'ardi fan-fudhuu laa tanfudhuuna 'illaa
bi-sulṭaan

فَبِأَيِّ آلَاءِ رَبِّكُمَا تُكَذِّبَانِ ﴿٣٤﴾

4. fa-bi-'ayyi 'aalaa'i Rabbikumaa
tukadhdhibaan

يُرْسَلُ عَلَيْكُمَا شُوَاظٌ مِّن نَّارٍ وَنُحَاسٌ فَلَا تَنتَصِرَانِ ﴿٣٥﴾

5. yursalu 'alaykumaa shawaaẓum min-naarin-
wa nuḥaasun fa-laa tan-taṣiraan

فَبِأَيِّ آلَاءِ رَبِّكُمَا تُكَذِّبَانِ ﴿٣٦﴾

6. fa-bi-'ayyi 'aalaaa'i Rabbikumaa
tukadhdhibaan

فَإِذَا انشَقَّتِ السَّمَاءُ فَكَانَتْ وَرْدَةً كَالدِّهَانِ ﴿٣٧﴾

37. fa-'idhanshaqqatis-samaaa'u fakaanat
wardatan kad-dihaan

فَبِأَيِّ آلَاءِ رَبِّكُمَا تُكَذِّبَانِ ﴿٣٨﴾

38. fa-bi-'ayyi 'aalaaa'i Rabbikumaa
tukadhdhibaan

فَيَوْمَئِذٍ لَّا يُسْأَلُ عَن ذَنبِهِ إِنسٌ وَلَا جَانٌّ ﴿٣٩﴾

39. fa-yawma'idhil laa yus'alu 'an dhanbihi
'insun-wa laa jaaann

فَبِأَيِّ آلَاءِ رَبِّكُمَا تُكَذِّبَانِ ﴿٤٠﴾

40. fa-bi-'ayyi 'aalaaa'i Rabbikumaa
tukadhdhibaan

41. (For) the sinners will be
Known by their Marks:
And they will be seized
By their forelocks and
Their feet.

42. Then which of the favours
Of your Lord will ye deny?

43. This is the Hell which
The Sinners deny:

44. In its midst
And in the midst
Of boiling hot water
Will they wander round!

45. Then which of the favours
Of your Lord will ye deny?

SECTION 3.

46. **B**ut for such as fear
The time when they will
Stand before (the Judgment Seat
Of) their Lord,
There will be two Gardens–

47. Then which of the favours
Of your Lord will ye deny?–

48. Abounding in
Branches;–

49. Then which of the favours
Of your Lord will ye deny?–

50. In them (each) will be
Two Springs flowing (free);

يُعْرَفُ الْمُجْرِمُونَ بِسِيمَاهُمْ فَيُؤْخَذُ بِالنَّوَاصِي وَالْأَقْدَامِ ﴿

. yu‘raful-mujrimuuna bi-siimaahum fa-
yu’khadhu bin-nawaaṣii wal-’aqdaam

فَبِأَيِّ آلَاءِ رَبِّكُمَا تُكَذِّبَانِ ﴿٤٢﴾

. fa-bi-’ayyı ’aalaaa’i Rabbikumaa
tukadhdhibaan

هَٰذِهِ جَهَنَّمُ الَّتِي يُكَذِّبُ بِهَا الْمُجْرِمُونَ ﴿٤٣﴾

. haadhihi jahannamul-latii yukadhdhibu
bihal-mujrimuun يَطُوفُونَ بَيْنَهَا وَبَيْنَ حَمِيمٍ آنٍ ﴿٤٤﴾

. yaṭuufuuna baynahaa wa bayna ḥamiimin
’aan

فَبِأَيِّ آلَاءِ رَبِّكُمَا تُكَذِّبَانِ ﴿٤٥﴾

. fa-bi-’ayyi ’aalaaa’i Rabbikumaa
tukadhdhibaan

وَلِمَنْ خَافَ مَقَامَ رَبِّهِ جَنَّتَانِ ﴿٤٦﴾

. wa-liman khaafa maqaama Rabbihi
jannataan

فَبِأَيِّ آلَاءِ رَبِّكُمَا تُكَذِّبَانِ ﴿٤٧﴾

. fa-bi-’ayyi ’aalaaa’i Rabbikumaa
tukadhdhibaan

ذَوَاتَا أَفْنَانٍ ﴿٤٨﴾

. dhawaataaa ’afnaan

فَبِأَيِّ آلَاءِ رَبِّكُمَا تُكَذِّبَانِ ﴿٤٩﴾

. fa-bi-’ayyi ’aalaaa’i Rabbikumaa
tukadhdhibáan

فِيهِمَا عَيْنَانِ تَجْرِيَانِ ﴿٥٠﴾

. fiihimaa ’aynaani tajriyaan

51. Then which of the favours
Of your Lord will ye deny?–

52. In them will be Fruits
Of every kind, two and two.

53. Then which of the favours
Of your Lord will ye deny?

54. They will recline on Carpets,
Whose inner linings will be
Of rich brocade: the Fruit
Of the Gardens will be
Near (and easy of reach).

55. Then which of the favours
Of your Lord will ye deny?

56. In them will be (Maidens),
Chaste, restraining their glances,
Whom no man or Jinn
Before them has touched;–

57. Then which of the favours
Of your Lord will ye deny?

58. Like unto rubies and coral.

59. Then which of the favours
Of your Lord will ye deny?

60. Is there any Reward
For Good–other than Good?

فَبِأَيِّ آلَاءِ رَبِّكُمَا تُكَذِّبَانِ ﴿٥١﴾

1. fa-bi-'ayyi 'aalaaa'i Rabbikumaa tukadhdhibaan

فِيهِمَا مِنْ كُلِّ فَاكِهَةٍ زَوْجَانِ ﴿٥٢﴾

2. fiihimaa min kulli faakihatin zawjaan

فَبِأَيِّ آلَاءِ رَبِّكُمَا تُكَذِّبَانِ ﴿٥٣﴾

3. fa-bi-'ayyi 'aalaa'i Rabbikumaa tukadhdhibaan

مُتَّكِئِينَ عَلَىٰ فُرُشٍ بَطَائِنُهَا مِنْ إِسْتَبْرَقٍ ۚ وَجَنَى الْجَنَّتَيْنِ دَانٍ ﴿٥٤﴾

4. muttaki'iina 'alla furushin baṭaaa'inuhaa ministabraq wa janal-jannatayni daan

فَبِأَيِّ آلَاءِ رَبِّكُمَا تُكَذِّبَانِ ﴿٥٥﴾

5. fa-bi-'ayyi 'aalaaa'i Rabbikumaa tukadhdhibban

فِيهِنَّ قَاصِرَاتُ الطَّرْفِ لَمْ يَطْمِثْهُنَّ إِنْسٌ قَبْلَهُمْ وَلَا جَانٌّ ﴿٥٦﴾

6. fiihinna qaaṣiraatuṭ-ṭarfi lam yaṭmithhunna 'insun qablahum wa laa jaaann

فَبِأَيِّ آلَاءِ رَبِّكُمَا تُكَذِّبَانِ ﴿٥٧﴾

7. fa-bi-'ayyi 'aalaaa'i Rabbikumaa tukadhdhibaan

كَأَنَّهُنَّ الْيَاقُوتُ وَالْمَرْجَانُ ﴿٥٨﴾

8. ka'annahunnal-yaaquutu wal-marjaan

فَبِأَيِّ آلَاءِ رَبِّكُمَا تُكَذِّبَانِ ﴿٥٩﴾

9. fa-bi-'ayyi 'aalaaa'i Rabbikumaa tukadhdhibaan

هَلْ جَزَاءُ الْإِحْسَانِ إِلَّا الْإِحْسَانُ ﴿٦٠﴾

0. hal jazaaa'ul-'iḥsaani 'illal-'iḥssan

61. Then which of the favours
Of your Lord will ye deny?

62. And besides these two,
There are two other Gardens,–

63. Then which of the favours
Of your Lord will ye deny?–

64. Dark-green in colour
(From plentiful watering).

65. Then which of the favours
Of your Lord will ye deny?

66. In them (each) will be
Two Springs pouring forth water
In continuous abundance:

67. Then which of the favours
Of your Lord will ye deny?

68. In them will be Fruits,
And dates and pomegranates:

69. Then which of the favours
Of your Lord will ye deny?

70. In them will be
Fair (Maidens), good, beautiful;–

فَبِأَيِّ آلَاءِ رَبِّكُمَا تُكَذِّبَانِ ﴿٦١﴾

1. fa-bi-'ayyi 'aalaaa'i Rabbikumaa tukadhdhibaan

وَمِن دُونِهِمَا جَنَّتَانِ ﴿٦٢﴾

2. wa min duunihimaa jannataan

فَبِأَيِّ آلَاءِ رَبِّكُمَا تُكَذِّبَانِ ﴿٦٣﴾

3. fa-bi-'ayyi 'aalaaa'i Rabbikumaa tukadhdhibaan

مُدْهَامَّتَانِ ﴿٦٤﴾

4. mud-haaammataan

فَبِأَيِّ آلَاءِ رَبِّكُمَا تُكَذِّبَانِ ﴿٦٥﴾

5. fa-bi-'ayyi 'aalaa'i Rabbikumaa tukadhdhibaan

فِيهِمَا عَيْنَانِ نَضَّاخَتَانِ ﴿٦٦﴾

6. fiihimaa 'aynaani naḍḍaakhataan

فَبِأَيِّ آلَاءِ رَبِّكُمَا تُكَذِّبَانِ ﴿٦٧﴾

7. fa-bi-'ayyi 'aalaaa'i Rabbikumaa tukadhdhibaan

فِيهِمَا فَاكِهَةٌ وَنَخْلٌ وَرُمَّانٌ ﴿٦٨﴾

8. fiihimaa faakihatuw-wa nakhluw-wa-rummaan

فَبِأَيِّ آلَاءِ رَبِّكُمَا تُكَذِّبَانِ ﴿٦٩﴾

9. fa-bi-'ayyi 'aalaaa'i Rabbikumaa tukadhdhibaan

فِيهِنَّ خَيْرَاتٌ حِسَانٌ ﴿٧٠﴾

0. fiihinna khayraatun ḥisaan

71. Then which of the favours
Of your Lord will ye deny?–

72. Maidens restrained (as to
Their glances), in (goodly)
pavilions:–

73. Then which of the favours
Of your Lord will ye deny?–

74. Whom no man or Jinn
Before them has touched;–

75. Then which of the favours
Of your Lord will ye deny?–

76. Reclining on green Cushions
And rich Carpets of beauty.

77. Then which of the favours
Of your Lord will ye deny?

78. Blessed be the name
Of thy Lord,
Full of Majesty,
Bounty and Honour.

فَبِأَيِّ آلَاءِ رَبِّكُمَا تُكَذِّبَانِ ﴿٧١﴾

. fa-bi-'ayyi 'aalaaa'i Rabbikumaa tukadhdhibaan

حُورٌ مَقْصُورَاتٌ فِي الْخِيَامِ ﴿٧٢﴾

. ḥuurum-maqṣuuraatun fil-khiyaam

فَبِأَيِّ آلَاءِ رَبِّكُمَا تُكَذِّبَانِ ﴿٧٣﴾

. fa-bi-'ayyi 'aalaaa'i Rabbikumaa tukadhdhibaan

لَمْ يَطْمِثْهُنَّ إِنْسٌ قَبْلَهُمْ وَلَا جَانٌّ ﴿٧٤﴾

. lam yaṭmithhunna 'insun qablahum wa laa jaaann

فَبِأَيِّ آلَاءِ رَبِّكُمَا تُكَذِّبَانِ ﴿٧٥﴾

. fa-bi-'ayyi 'aalaaa'i Rabbikumaa tukadhdhibaan

مُتَّكِئِينَ عَلَىٰ رَفْرَفٍ خُضْرٍ وَعَبْقَرِيٍّ حِسَانٍ ﴿٧٦﴾

. muttaki'iina 'allaa rafrafin khuḍrin-wa 'abqariyyin ḥisaan

فَبِأَيِّ آلَاءِ رَبِّكُمَا تُكَذِّبَانِ ﴿٧٧﴾

. fa-bi-'ayyi 'aalaaa'i Rabbikumaa tukadhdhibaan

تَبَارَكَ اسْمُ رَبِّكَ ذِي الْجَلَالِ وَالْإِكْرَامِ ﴿٧٨﴾

. tabaarakasmu Rabbika Dhil-jalaali wal-'ikraam

يس

Yā-Sin and Al-Rahmān

وَ

الرَّحْمٰنُ

مكتبة
DAR AL TAQWA LTD
دار التقوى